LUCK OF THE DRAW

Piano/Vocal Arrangements by
    Mark Phillips
Music Engraving by
    Gordon Hallberg
Art Direction:
    Kerstin Fairbend
Administration:
    Daniel Rosenbaum
Director of Music:
    Mark Phillips
Photography by
    Merlyn Rosenberg

ISBN: 0-89524-646-5

Edited by Milton Okun

Finale notation software was used to engrave the compositions in this book.

CoNTENTs

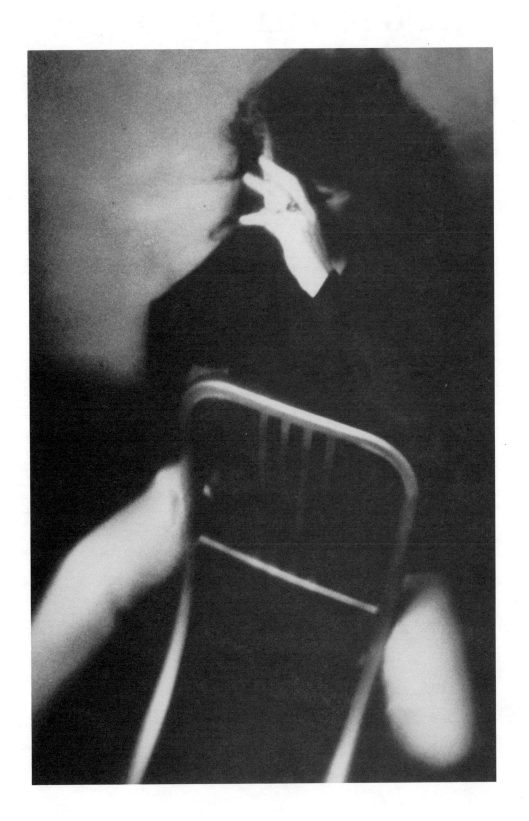

SOMETHING TO TALK ABOUT

Words and Music by
Shirley Eikhard

Moderate Reggae/Rock

Peo - ple are talk - ing, talk - ing 'bout peo - ple. I nev - er no - ticed

I feel so fool - ish,

I hear them whis - per, you won't be - lieve it.

you'd act so nerv - ous. Could you be fall - ing for me?

They think we're lov - ers kept un - der - cov - er.

It took a ru - mor to make me won - der.

* Recorded a half step lower

7

Let's give them some-thing to talk a-bout.
Let's give them some-thing to talk a-bout,

Let's give them some-thing to talk a-bout.
a lit-tle mys-t'ry to fig-ure out.

Let's give them some-thing to talk a-bout. How a-bout love?
Let's give them some-thing to talk a-bout. How a-bout love,

love, love?

Let's give them some-thing to talk a-bout,

a lit-tle mys-t'ry to fig-ure out.____

Let's give them some-thing to talk a-bout. How a-bout love?____

Repeat and fade

GOOD MAN, GOOD WOMAN

Words and Music by
C. Womack and L. Womack

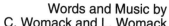

Medium Funk/Rock

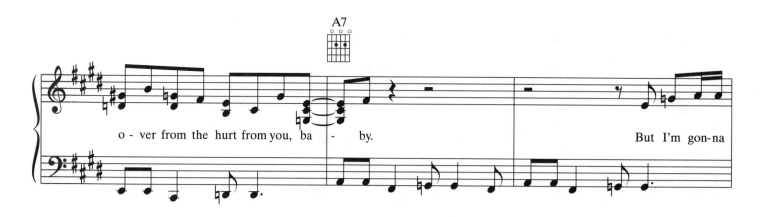

up, you were al-read-y gone. I

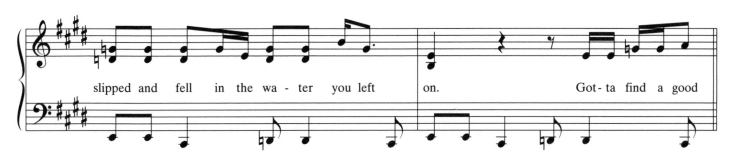

slipped and fell in the wa-ter you left on. Got-ta find a good

E7

wom-an. Gon-na find a good man. I got-ta find a good

Repeat and fade

wom-an. I'm gon-na find a good man. Got-ta find a good

Additional Lyrics

2. You better stop and think about what you're saying.
I was seriously dedicated in this game we're playin'.
You made ten thousand promises you couldn't keep.
I forgave you when you lied, pleaded and weeped,
I put up with your disrespect and neglect.
It was an experience I'll never forget.
Till now, everything I did was wrong. Sorry, baby.
Today we're free, but we live alone.
Gotta find a good woman, good woman, good woman, yeah, yeah, yeah.

I CAN'T MAKE YOU LOVE ME

Words and Music by
M. Reid and A. Shamblin

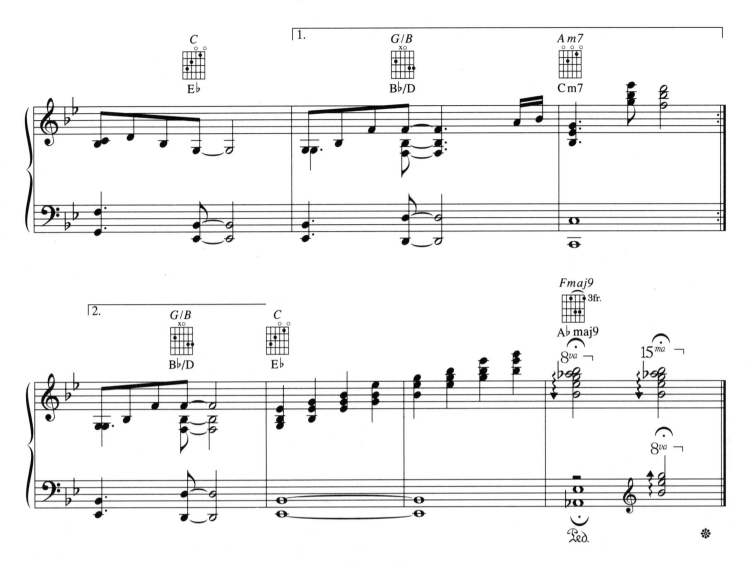

Additional Lyrics

2. I'll close my eyes, then I won't see
   The love you don't feel when you're holdin' me.
   Mornin' will come and I'll do what's right.
   Just give me till then to give up this fight.
   And I will give up this fight. *(To Chorus)*

TANGLED AND DARK

Words and Music by
Bonnie Raitt

down where your fears are— parked.——

Gon-na tell the truth a-bout it,— babe.——

Hon-ey, that's the hard-est— part.——

When we get through it, ba-by,———

gon-na give up your heart.———

Additional Lyrics

2. Gonna get into it, baby.
   Gonna give them demons a call.
   Way on into it, baby,
   Gonna find out once and for all.
   Gonna get a little risky, baby.
   Honey, that's my favorite part.
   When we get through it, baby,
   Gonna give up our hearts,
   Gonna give up our hearts. *(To Bridge)*

3. *Repeat 1st Verse*

NO BUSINESS

Words and Music by
John Hiatt

1. Yes, I'm lone - ly; hope you don't catch____ it.

2.3. *See additional lyrics*

Don't want to be down where I last be - haved.____

I broke his heart;___ now I can - not patch___ it. This___ time it's

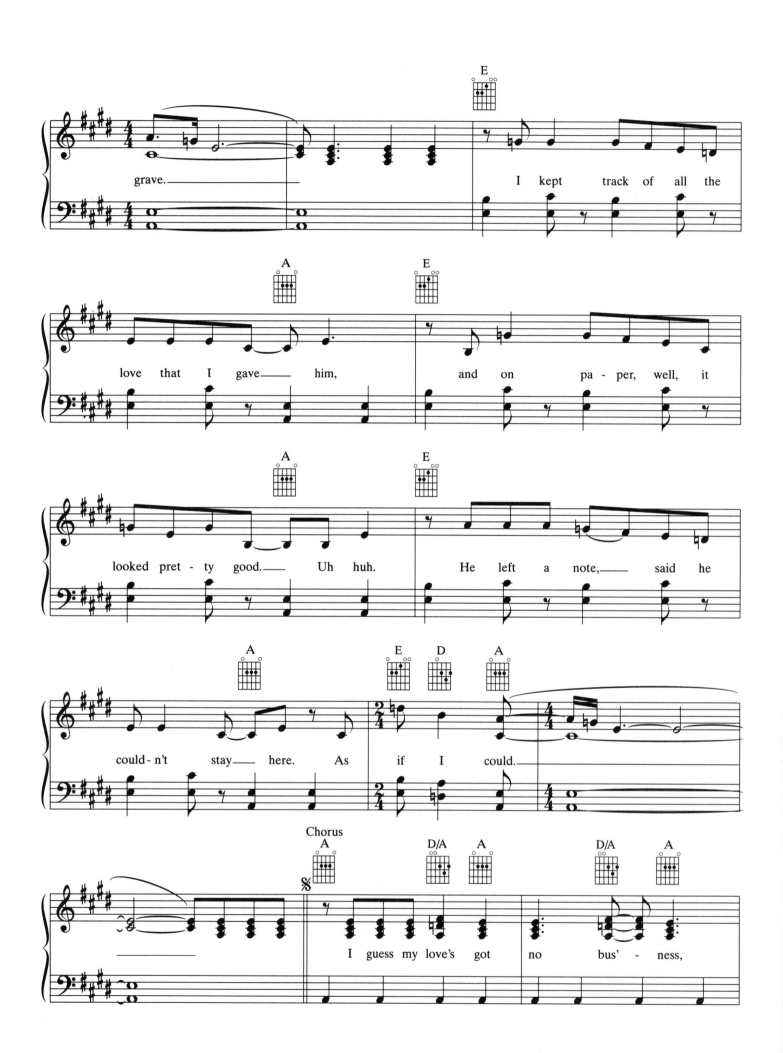

grave.

I kept track of all the love that I gave him, and on pa - per, well, it looked pret - ty good. Uh huh. He left a note, said he could - n't stay here. As if I could.

Chorus

I guess my love's got no bus' - ness,

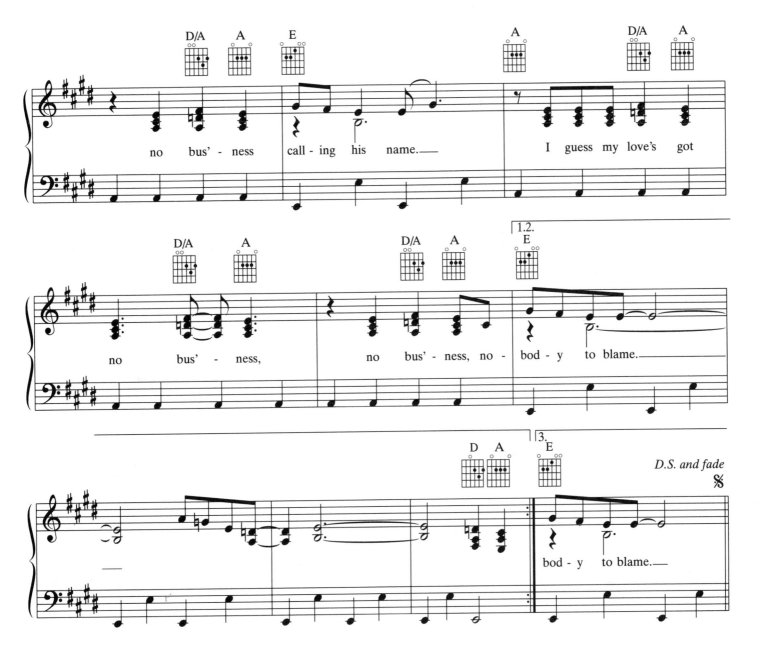

Additional Lyrics

2. One of these days I thought we'd get it together.
   After all, that boy was made for me.
   But all he left me was a mouth full of feathers.
   Little bird got free.
   He always said my love was one-sided.
   I tried to keep up with supply and demand.
   But there was one way that pie was divided.
   It was a big piece plan. *(To Chorus)*

3. Well, now I'm getting desperate, getting illegal.
   I got them law doggies on my trail.
   The hawk's out and I could use an eagle
   To go my bail.
   You say you're itching, baby; go ahead and scratch it.
   But if it jumps off, don't you look at me.
   You swore to God, baby, I couldn't catch it,
   But this dog got fleas. *(To Chorus)*

COME TO ME

Words and Music by
Bonnie Raitt

Moderate Raggae/Rock

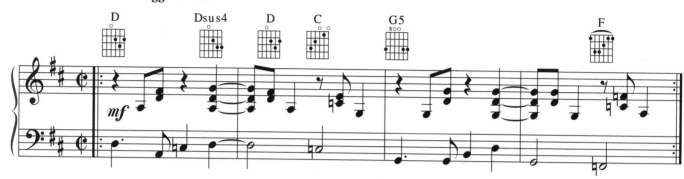

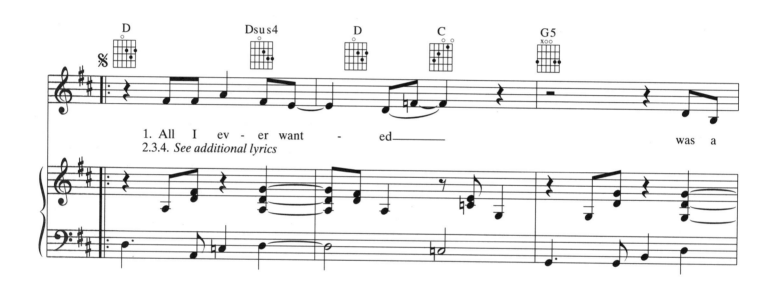

1. All I ev - er want - ed_____ was a
2.3.4. *See additional lyrics*

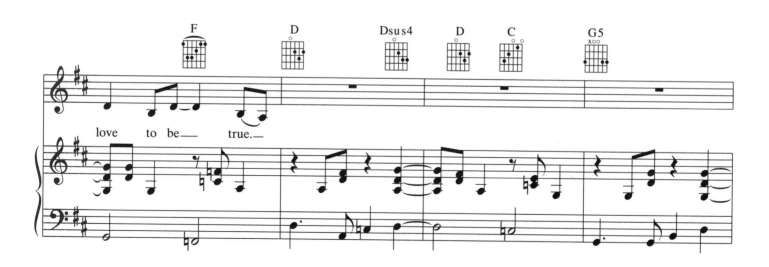

love to be___ true.___

Additional Lyrics

2. I don't need another well-spent night,
   Another clever, sideways glance.
   I wanna look my baby in the eye
   And know there's nothin' left to chance. *(To Chorus)*

3. Well, I'm gonna hold out for the one I want.
   Ain't gonna settle for less.
   'Cause the kind of love I'm lookin' for, baby,
   You can't fake, you can't finesse.

4. I ain't lookin' for the kind of man, baby,
   Can't stand a little shaky ground.
   He'll give me fire and tenderness
   And got the guts to stick around. *(To Chorus)*

ONE PART BE MY LOVER

Words and Music by
Bonnie Raitt and Michael O'Keefe

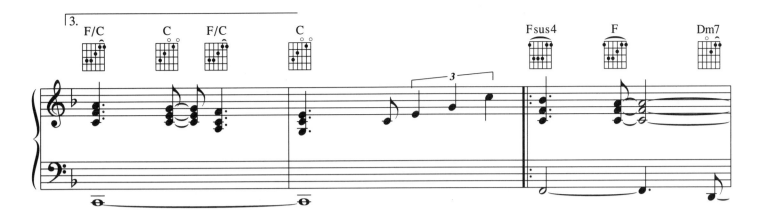

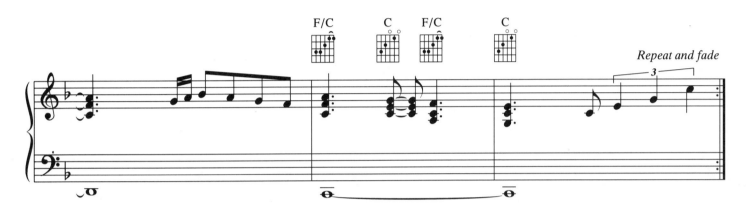

Additional Lyrics

2. He's like a boxer who had to retire
   After winning but killing a man.
   All of the moves and none of the courage,
   Afraid to throw a punch that might land.
   Not too much later she can't meet his glance.
   You see her start pulling away.
   Over and over like fire and ice,
   One is color, one is grey.
   They're not forever, just for today.
   One part be my lover, one part go away.

3. If you know how, why don't you say 'em a prayer,
   They're gonna need all the help they can get.
   They remember too much about what went wrong.
   It might be they should learn to forget.
   Forget themselves in each other
   And leave what belongs in the past,
   Carry their hearts like a newborn child,
   'Cause it's only the moment that lasts.
   They're not forever, just day to day.
   One part be my lover, one part go away.

NOT THE ONLY ONE

Words and Music by
Paul Brady

Medium Pop

I was in a daze,_____ mov-in' in the wrong di - rec-

tion, feel-in' that I'd al - ways_____ be the lone-

B♭sus2

F

ly one._____

1.2. Then I saw your face
3. When I saw your face

on the edge of my ho - ri - zon,
through the web of my con - fu - sion,

whis - per - in' that

B♭sus2

I was - n't the___ on - ly one,_____

To Coda ⊕

Dm

the lone - ly one._____

Gm7 3fr.

C/D

Gm7 3fr.

One chance in - ter - ven - tion,_____
True love or per - fec - tion,_____

see what it can sig - ni - fy._____
it seems like it's o - ver - due._____

SLOW RIDE

Words and Music by
Bonnie Hayes, Andre Pessis
and Larry John McNally

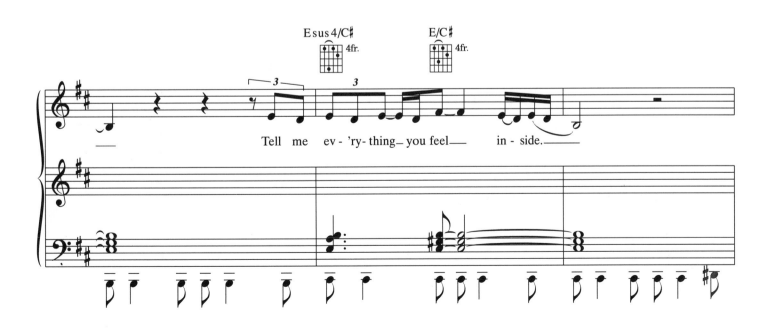

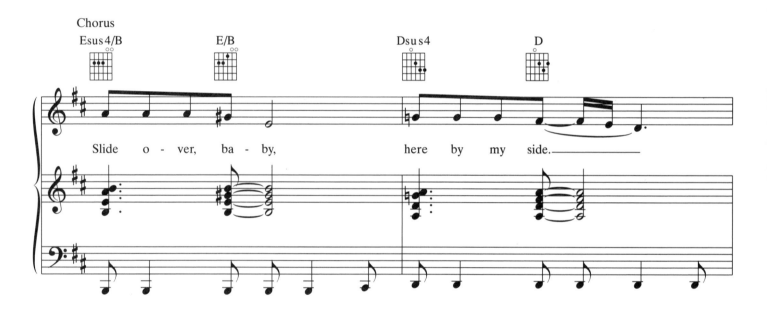

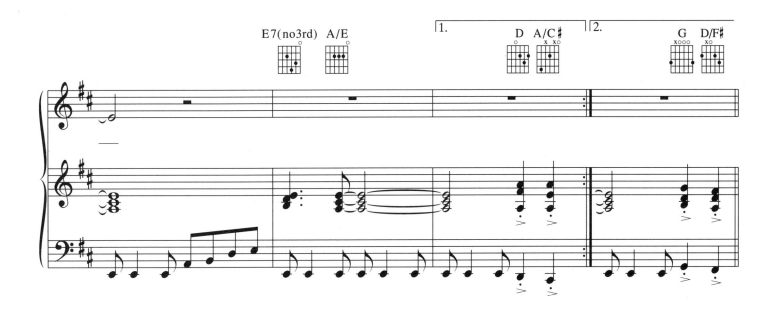

Additional Lyrics

2. Your history shows on your face.
   Yeah, you've been hurt, you've been betrayed.
   Now, we can't change the past, but we can
   Leave it behind.
   We'll forget about tomorrow, baby.
   We'll just steal away into the night.
   And we'll just be two shadows, darlin,
   In the dashboard light. *(To Chorus)*

LUCK OF THE DRAW

Words and Music by
Paul Brady

PAPA COME QUICK *(JODY AND CHICO)*

Words and Music by
B. Vera, C. Taylor
and R. Hirsch

let's haul ass_____ be - fore the ba - by gets burned.

Gas up the old Ford, get out the road map. They

got a head start a - bout a half a day. Load up the shot - gun,

put it in the gun - rack. Jo - dy's with Chi - co down in East L.____ A.____

Stop at the Mo - bil, pump up the flat wheel. Jo - dy and Chi - co and his

E   E

ding dang— deal.—

B   E

B   E

Ma -

E

Tacet

ma's been cry - in' in the kitch - en since morn - in'. She cried right through As The

World——— Turns.——— Seen it my-self,——— and Pa - pa, it's a bitch, 'n'

let's haul ass——— be - fore the ba - by gets burned.

ALL AT ONCE

Words and Music by
Bonnie Raitt

Moderately slow

1. Had a fight with my daugh-ter;⎯⎯⎯ she flew off⎯ in a rage.

2.3. *See additional lyrics*

Third time this week; don't tell me it's the age.⎯⎯⎯

Additional Lyrics

2. Ah, who am I kiddin'?
   I should have known he'd never leave.
   The time we spend together
   Is harder than the time between.
   You wouldn't think it could hurt so
   To see 'em out the other day.
   If that's what he calls leavin',
   I guess I threw it all away. *(To Chorus)*

3. They say women, we're the stronger,
   Somehow we always make it through.
   Hell, that ain't what I feel right now;
   I don't even think it's true.
   Looks to me there's lots more broken
   Than anyone can really see.
   Why the angels turn their backs on some,
   It's a mystery to me. *(To Chorus)*

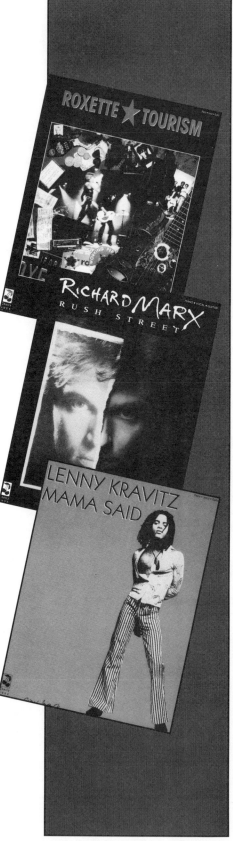